April 28, 2007

A Blessing,
Caring & Sharing

May the sunshine
upon your Ead
day.

Doris Washington
Poet

A Blessing, Caring & Sharing

Poems By

Doris Washington

To order additional copies of this book, contact:
Xlibris Corporation
1-888-795-4274
www.Xlibris.com
Orders@Xlibris.com
24288

Contents

A New Day

New Life

Dedication

To My husband John who is that anchor of support and my best friend. You have been that anchor of support always, and a friend that comes along once in a lifetime. I cherish our life together. God bless you for your love.

To my son, John, you are my inspiration to write, a gift from God. My life is so fulfilled with you in it. Your inspiration made this creation of work all possible. And much more than that, you have taught me how to Love.

To my dear friends Pricilla Gallegos and Bishop Clara Elliott. Thank you for your love and support always. Thank you for just being there.

To Nathaniel Gadsden and friends of the Writers Wordshop, you were a building block for me. Thank you for always making a place for Writers to grow.

To many friends and family, your support, your encouragement means more than you know. God bless you for it. God bless you for your love.

Acknowledgements

I would like to acknowledge my husband John Washington Jr., Ann Neimer, Neal Carrigan, Bishop Clara E. Elliott, Reverend Barbara Walker, Ira Bolden Jr., Shaashawn Dial, Bob & Debbie Ryder, Alda Hanna, Loretta Barbee—Dare, Afi Roberson, Anthony Watson, Angela Lundy and many friends and poets for their support and encouragement in helping to make this creation of work possible.

Foreword

My son John is my inspiration to write. John has taught me what love is all about. Living with Autism has helped me see that everyone has their own unique gift to offer to the world. We are all different, and yet we are all the same. Because of John I have been inspired to write poems of many dimensions. I have found my closeness with God. Inner peace I practice in my life daily. I pray always for peace in our world. I hope this book will touch at least one person's life, and as it does that, may it be an inspiration to many.

RISING ABOVE THE STORM

The Lord's Grace

There's nothing like the Lord's Grace.
A feeling within your soul—a journey to the right place.

A feeling of negativity to no longer enter your mind.
True goodness, righteousness, and always love you will find.

For no matter where you are, His Love is always around.
And with His Love, it lifts you up in spirit, you're heavenly bound.

It is a journey towards true salvation for the rest of your days.
For the Lord's Grace is a feeling of Love in your heart always.
For there's nothing like-
The Lord's Grace

The Lord Watches Over Me

I do not fear the darkness at night.
For the sparrow stays within my sight.
Oh! How The Lord Watches Over Me.

I do not fear the arrows that come at me
during the day.
For the Lord is all around,
He is with me in every way.
The Lord Watches Over Me.

I do not dwell too long in despair.
For I know I am in the Lord's care.
The Lord He Watches Over Me.

I trust in the Lord, I hold on to his
unchanging hand.
For when I am weak, he helps me stand.
The Lord Watches Over Me.

I will stay in the house of the Lord,
He will never leave me.
For I know with Faith,
He is with me, through eternity!
Oh! How The Lord Watches Over Me.

Rising Above The Storm

The problems keep coming, and don't seem
to go away.
I feel so tired, ready to quit, and still I pray.
I pray to weather the Storm as the tide rises so high.
And when I know I've done all I can,
I find comfort to know I tried.

So I Stand! And I Stand!
For the Lord gives me strength to get through.
And when the days seem cloudy and gray,
I don't carry the blues.
So I pray, and trust in the Lord to know
He will always be there.
And as the tide rises so high,
my burdens are not heavy to bear.
Rising Above The Storm

Road Blocks

As I keep going each day,
I am finding many Road Blocks along the way.

Whether I go left or right.
Going forward—traveling day or night.

The Road Blocks are always there.
Feeling helpless, and in despair.

Frustrated! Not knowing what to do,
I remember that Prayer is the answer,
and I come to know the Lord will see me through.

And as I journey on—I continue on with
the many Road Blocks along the way.
And again, I remember to Pray.

For the Lord is never forsaking.
He gives me strength, and I stay strong.
And as he sees me through—I continue on.
For there are many-
Road Blocks

My Blues

Broken Dreams
Many Disappointments
Closed Doors
Delayed Goals
Long Suffering
Undue Financial Burdens
Overworked, and Not Enough Pay
Insufficient Love
Inconsideration
Less Time to Breathe
Too Much Discrimination
Racial Profiling
Disability Rights Overlooked
Not Enough Diversity
Families Drifting Away
Poor Health Care
Lack of Education
Many Hungry People
Children Dying
A Mother's Cry
My Blues

A Mother's Love

A Mother's Love is behind her struggles, and strife.
A Mother's Love never ends as she goes through
joyous, sad, and disappointing times in her life.

A Mother's Love is when her child hurts, for as
her child hurts, so does she.
And she asks the question: "How could this be?"

For she must be strong, as she endures all things.
And through her endurance, such a Blessing
it brings.

A Mother's Love is the pride she feels, when her
child does not stray.
A Mother's Love is warm in every way.

A Mother's Love is constant, and dear.
A Mother's Love is understanding, and she
is always near.

For there's nothing like A Mother's Love. "Can't you see?"
A Mother's Love, compassionate, understanding, and dear.
Oh! How Loving It Can Be!

I BEAT AT A DRUM

The Child That Plays Alone

He talks to himself, and no one hears what he says.
His activity seems strange and unusual to some.

If only they would see his gift, he could accomplish
more than you know.
If only someone would take the time to explore
what he has.

He could be a great musician, a great artist, a great dancer-
a great athlete.
He has many toys, and he plays by himself.
The other children do not understand him.
They do not play with him.

He likes to do the same things other children do.
And yet he is shut out from the world.
He is different, but aren't we all different.

If only someone would play with him.
If only someone would see His Gift!
The Child That Plays Alone

Do You See Him? Do You Hear Him? Do You Know Him?

Do You See Him? He is my child,
And he is dear to me.
He has Autism, an Invisible Disability.

Do You Hear Him? You may not understand
why he does not quickly respond to you.
For he is not bad,
He is just different from what you are used to.

Do you Know Him? You may find
he will need more time to do a certain task.
And if there are too many demands,
please understand they may be difficult
for him to grasp.

For there are other places,
I could have chose for him to live.
I made the choice for him to stay with me.
For I see what he can give.

He may not understand danger.
I worry if he will be safe.
And as I struggle with the many difficulties,
and challenges—"I Keep The Faith!"

I only ask for him—One Request.
Please Learn About Him.
So he can have a chance to give His Best!
Do You See Him? Do You Hear Him? Do You Know Him?

I Beat At A Drum

I Beat At A Drum you're not familiar with.
For the Lord blesses each of us with a Gift.

I make a sound you may not understand.
I have the humbleness to be someone's friend.

I Beat At A Drum you're not familiar with.
For the Lord blesses each of us with a gift.

I can memorize dates to be exact.
I was born this way, for that is a fact.

I Beat At A Drum you're not familiar with.
For the Lord blesses each of us with a Gift.

I can use my skills to work at a job productively.
I just need a little assistance from those in my community.

I Beat At A Drum you're not familiar with.
For the Lord blesses each of us with a Gift.

You may hear a sound different from what you have known.
Please Hear and Listen.
For the Lord makes room for everyone.
I Beat At A Drum!

John

You are a precious child.
For you have been sent from God above.
You are the joy of my life.
For you have taught me how to Love.

You brighten up the day with your everlasting smile.
I am so proud to have you as my son.
For you help make my life worthwhile.

As I hear your sweet melody of songs you sing.
It could be a spiritual or popular tune or too.
How beautiful and special you are.
For this is all-What makes You!

You make my life worth living.
And I keep going each and everyday.
How important you are to me—So true!
As I look forward to everyday,
And I hear you say: "God is with us."
And I respond, "All the time."
I could not imagine my life without you.
My Precious Son—
John

PRAYER POEM FOR PEACE

Can We Stop And Take A Minute?

Is anybody here?
Can you hear me?
Things sure have changed.
Can we stop and take a minute to really talk to one another?

And how busy we are with so many things.
Whether it's getting on our jobs,
and with the hurry up and go,
and taking care of our families,
and with the other projects we may have,
there just seems not enough hours in the day.
But-
Can we stop and take a minute to listen and appreciate what life
is really all about?

Can we stop and take a minute to give a "friendly greeting" to someone,
and wish them well, as we go through our busy day?
Can we stop and take a minute to enjoy a beautiful song, or a poem,
and maybe watch a good movie?

Can we stop and take a minute to give someone a "friendly smile,"
And offer encouragement, even when we may feel bad?
Can we stop and take a minute to notice when someone is sad,
to just uplift them with love in our heart?

Can we stop and take a minute when someone takes the time
to offer a hand of kindness, we can do the same for them?
Can we stop and take a minute to spend some time with friends,
and love ones?

And can we stop, and take a minute to enjoy life's precious moments.
For life is not promised to us.
Can We Stop And Take A Minute?

Walls

Walls divide us, separate us, keep us away.
Love has no place to stay.

Walls limit us to only go so far.
They stagnate us from being who we are.

Walls promote ignorance, and encourage
discrimination.
Differences are not welcomed, leaving not
much room for communication.

Walls block understanding from coming in.
They breathe prejudice outwardly, and within.

Walls keep our spirits dormant.
They do not allow us to trust.
They close our hearts to where we don't give
the best of us.

Walls—Divide! Divide! Divide!
And behind them we hide.

Walls—For if we bring them down.
Love! Love! Love!—will stay around.
Walls!

Prayer Poem For Peace

May God give us Peace each day through our troubled World.

May God give us Strength to endure the trials,
and struggles from day to day.

May God give us Refuge, release our fears, our anxieties,
when there's danger and distress.

May God give us Comfort where's there's suffering and despair.

May God give us Joy to live each moment, to cherish the blessings
He grants us around every corner.

May God give us Guidance to live each day productively, and whole.

May God give us Faith to know He is always there day and night.

May God give us Hope to live for a better tomorrow-
opening up our hearts—to His Love.

May God give us Peace each day through our troubled World.
May God Give Us Peace

His Dream

Long ago, there was a man, who had a Dream.
A dream for everyone to live together in harmony.
All races, creed, gender, disability, and nationality.

He spoke as the way he lived.
Standing for Truth! Justice! Liberty!
For all of us to be free.
As we remember him, we are reminded of what
He tried to do-
to make it a better place for you and me.

His message was so simple.
To show each other the act of Love.
For we must all do our part.
Oh! How wonderful it could be
if we can continue His Dream-
in our heart.

For He Lives! "I Have A Dream" he said.
And so it must be.
For one day His Dream to be realized,
for us to live out the meaning of what is so true.
For all of us to be—free!
We Must Continue-
His Dream

Choices

We can choose to be negative,
or we can choose to be positive.
We can live in darkness, or we
can turn on the light if we so choose.

We can choose to follow our dreams,
or we can choose not to.
We can limit ourselves to go only so far,
or we can seek our desires to endless
possibilities if we so choose.

We can make our own truth with
jealousy, envy, and paranoia,
or we can open our minds to
the truth if we so choose.

We can choose to be at war,
or we can choose to be at peace.
We can harvest the seeds of ignorance and hate,
or we can harvest the seeds of love if we so choose.

We choose the directions we take in our lives!
We choose the directions we take in our lives!
We Make Our Own-
Choices!

All Of A Sudden

Children will no longer be killing children.
All Of A Sudden

Families will spend more time together, not apart.
All Of A Sudden

People will start to talk, and not argue.
All Of A Sudden

Police will serve and protect all their citizens,
no matter race or disability.
All Of A Sudden

There will be no more hunger in the land.
All Of A Sudden

There will be a cure for cancer, and the sick will
have hope.
All Of A Sudden

All of us will have a better quality of life.
All Of A Sudden

There will be no more hate, only love.
For before you know it—God's Love
will conquer all.
All Of A Sudden!

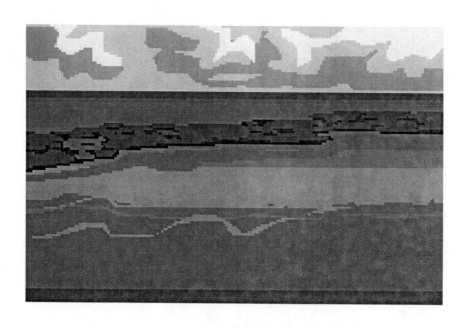

A NEW DAY

I Do Not Want To Hurt Anymore

I'm afraid.
Why?
I have been hurt.
And it seems as though
things don't change.
What to do?

I feel at times I want to go away,
and hide.
Still I find that is not the answer.

Should I just avoid situations
with those who can be cruel?
Still I find that is not the answer.

Should I just cry?
Oh! but that would make me sad.
And I have been there before.
Or should I just be mad?
And I have been there before too.
And I was unhappy.
And yet, I'm still afraid.
So I pray! And I pray! And I pray!

Maybe if I just learn to like myself.
I may come to see that I am someone.
Then maybe I can believe everything
will be just fine.
For-
I Do Not Want To Hurt Anymore

Accepting

Healing from the hurt and pain,
I cry no tears like rain.
I Am—Accepting

Letting go of things that don't change.
Cleaning out the junk in my heart-
only to rearrange.
I Am—Accepting

To Rearrange! To Rearrange!
Putting things in priority.
Seeing Blessings,
And no excess baggage I carry.
I Am—Accepting

Moving away from disappointments.
Picking up the broken pieces to begin again.
Never giving up on life.
Loving who I am.
Believing I am my best friend.
I Am—Accepting

Not wearing a frown.
Carrying only a smile.
Giving my worries to God.
And all the while-
I Am-
Accepting

A New Day

I awake from a long sleep, yes a long sleep
from loneliness, self pity, and regret.
I no longer choose to taste the bitter tongue of
the trials of life.

I no longer allow worry, self-doubt, and
negative energy to be the focus of existence.
I no longer starve for others approval, opinions, and love.

Forgiveness is what I practice.
Patience has become my daily routine.
Love keeps me alive.
And I seek Him always.
As I Start-
A New Day

Gathering Stones

Recovering from it all,
I pick up the broken pieces
along the way.
Drifting away far too long,
I now re-group, to get some balance.
And I'm ready to begin again.

There's so much out here
to discover.
And yet I feel uncertain where
I'm going.
Taking it one step at a time,
I seek the desires of my heart.
And my dreams are not far away
to be fulfilled.

Recovering from it all,
I pick up the scattered pieces
along the way.
Drifting away far too long,
I now re-group, to get some balance.
And I'm ready to begin again.
Out Here-
Gathering Stones

Alone

Alone does not always stand for lonely,
Sometimes it's a great healing, that space
to grow.

Alone sometimes helps you with a great
sense of focus and perspective.
And the trials can be triumphs.

Alone sometimes helps you stay encouraged,
empowering you to many heights, many possibilities.

Alone is a period each of us experiences for however
long it may be.
Overcoming barriers, moving forward with belief
in one's self.

Alone does not always stand for lonely.
For it can take you to other places, expanding
your horizons,
and finding you're not-
Alone

Assumptions

Assumptions can cause you to make a choice
that's not always the best.
And that choice you make may leave you with regret.

For Assumptions leads you to an avenue to miss
something of great importance you let pass by.
Which may leave you wondering later: What if? and Why?

Assumptions will block Blessings that do come your way.
For with Assumptions you can only experience the ordinary
from day to day.

And Assumptions will cause you to have an opinion of
someone that is not always good.
With Assumptions you may miss a good friendship, a great love.
And you are left asking later: Should I have? And only if I could?

Follow your vibes if you must.
Just make sure you are not ruled with Assumptions to not trust.

Remember to not always make Assumptions about a situation,
or someone.
Keep an open mind, and never loose sight.
For with Assumptions—you may miss more than you like.
Just Examine your-
Assumptions

Don't Forget To Count

Your Blessings

When at times things are not going right.
Just remember to hold on to the good things in your life.
Don't Forget To Count Your Blessings

When there are those you find do not think of you.
Remember the ones who do.
Don't Forget To Count Your Blessings

When you find the world is not kind.
Look for the "rainbow" in the sky, and know
you will be fine.
Don't Forget To Count Your Blessings

And when you cannot find what you are looking for.
Look around,
And be thankful the Lord has for You-
greater things in store.
Don't Forget To Count Your Blessings!

NEW LIFE

The Wilderness

Darkness surrounded me, I could not find the light.
The Light was there, but I could not see it.
Assumptions of what I perceived, became my reality.
Negative energy kept coming in when I least expected.

Loneliness, bitterness, and despair engulfed my spirit,
I could not breathe.
Then a voice said: "Come With Me."
He talked to me there.
He guided me to a place of peacefulness
that I've never known.
There were many trees to guide me along the way.

They were marked with directions to where
I was meant to be.
I then began to see the light through the darkness.
The Blessings that were always there,
I began to see, and receive.

His Love filled me! His Love engulfed me!
Positive thoughts became my reality.
I was no longer misguided.
The place I was meant to be was not far.
With Him I was not alone.
For with His Light-
He saw me through-
The Wilderness

You

Silence after the Storm,
the Storm that was raging
so long.
The Storm is over now.
Time to start a new direction.
Time to find a new sense of
purpose.
Leaving what is familiar,
even with new ventures to seek,
the old will not be again.
And taking it one step at a time,
it will be alright.
For I'm here,
alive like I never been before.
Thank you Lord!
I begin here!
I begin with-
You!

New Life

As I move towards a new way of thinking-
positive—leaving all old habits of negativity
behind me,
I discover new oceans with a sense of direction.
Going forward I can plainly see the sunset-
the blue skies.

Oh! How beautiful it is to see God's creation.
For life is so precious to waste
even a minute of it's treasure's to go by.

As I stop and take time to smell the roses,
I have a smile on my face,
with Love in my heart for others.
For this I must try.

In knowing I can always begin again,
in an effort towards being the best I can be.
To seek salvation,
To live a better way.

And as I find I have complete serenity
within my heart.
For then I can say-
This is a wonderful-
New Life

Take Me To Your Place

Touch me My Father!
Shower me with your goodness, and grace.
Help me stay still in times of trouble,
and for whatever trials I may face.
Take Me To Your Place

Strengthen me in the Spirit, so your voice
is the only voice I hear.
Stay with me, and talk to me, whether it be far or near.
Take Me To Your Place

Anoint me! Lift me up in your spirit!
Help me accept and love others for who they are.
Grant me everlasting peace.
And if I stray Lord too far!-
Take Me To Your Place

Faith

It keeps you going forward.
With it—opportunities are yours to explore.
You can follow the desires deep within you.
You can overcome the barriers—the obstacles.
You can cross bridges that seem so far to reach.
You can climb any mountain.
And like an eagle you can fly high above the skies-
With Courage-
With Confidence-
With Strength-
With-
Faith

On My Journey

On My Journey
I've traveled many places, and I've learned
so much, and yet—I'm still learning.

On My Journey
I've experienced disappointments, as well as triumphs.
I've found me, and I'm happy with what I've found.

On My Journey
I've found that things can change, even with the same
situation, and that nothing is complete, or certain.

On My Journey
I've discovered that no matter what others opinions may be,
one has to make choices which is best for them.

On My Journey
I've opened my mind to see the goodness in others,
letting go of what I can't change.
Finding where I need to be.

On My Journey
I've traveled many places, and I've learned
so much, and yet-
I'm still learning

Changing

Things may be routine, but don't always
remain the same.
A sudden occurrence can happen when
least expected.

Like a Detour, one's life can turn in a
different direction.
But no matter, one moves on, for one must.
And if dreams are deferred, one must hold
on to them.
For they can still come true.

And one must be happy with the choices they've
chosen.
Not content, but happy.
For life itself is a Blessing.
And the world is forever-
Changing

New

Each day is New.
Days passed are preparations
for what's ahead.
Each day you can always
start over.
And as you awake, you have
a chance to do what you
did not do before.
You have a chance to change
it all around.
For it starts with one person.
And as one does it, it can
encourage others to do the same.
Just think about it.
For each day is-
New

Love

It's everywhere.
It solves every problem.
It resolves conflict.
It makes a way for every solution.
It doesn't discriminate or judge.
It brings people together.
We can't live without it.
We may turn away from it.
We may cover it over with things.
And sometimes we may not see
it when it comes.
But-
If we step back, we can see it so clear.
We can see it through the smiles and the hugs.
We can see it through encouragement.
We can see it through a listening ear.
We can see it through the support of a friend,
especially when we need it the most.
We can see it through patience, and understanding.
We can see it through kindness, and compassion.
Yes, we can see it!
It's Everywhere!
It's-
Love!

Printed in the United States
63139LVS00004B/22-111